Introduction

One of the side effects of quilting is the ever-growing stash and scraps that seem to appear like magic. It seems, as quilters, we tend to buy a bit extra "just in case," or we cut something wrong but the fabric is just too gorgeous to toss. So, we start a scrap basket or a drawer for the extras. Sometimes we simply buy a beautiful piece of fabric with no project in mind, and so it joins the stash. After a few months or years we notice that what was once a small basket or drawer has turned into an entire sewing room full of beautiful fabrics waiting for a project.

Well *Stash-Busting Quilts* will become your go-to book for inspiration when cleaning out your stash. With nine creative patterns designed with stash and scraps in mind, you can't go wrong. Some of our most talented designers have put forth their best efforts and this collection was born. This is the book you'll want to keep handy when you feel the urge to clean, organize and use your stashed treasures.

This book has something for everyone—quilts in all sizes and table runners in all styles. All you need is stash and the desire to use it.

Table of Contents

Village by the Sea

Slice your way through the scraps in your stash to stitch up these easy blocks and create a fun beach community.

Design by Lyn Brown
Quilted by Cathy O'Brien

Skill Level
Confident Beginner

Specifications
Quilt Size: 70" x 86"
Block Sizes: 6" x 16" finished and 4" x 16" finished
Number of Blocks: 24 and 12

Materials
- Assorted batik scraps for houses in blue, green, purple, pink, gold, teal, yellow and orange
- Assorted red batik scraps
- 3⅛ yards white batik
- Backing to size
- Batting to size
- Thread
- Basic sewing tools and supplies

Project Notes
Read all instructions before beginning this project.

Stitch right sides together using a ¼" seam allowance unless otherwise specified.

Materials and cutting lists assume 40" of usable fabric width for yardage.

Cutting

From assorted batik scraps for houses:
- Cut 12 (5½" x 6½") G rectangles.
- Cut 12 matching sets of 1 each 5½" x 6½" E rectangle and 3⅞" F square.
- Cut 12 (3½" x 6½") J rectangles.
- Cut 12 matching sets of 1 each 3½" x 6½" H rectangle and 3⅞" I square.
- Cut 12 (4½") N squares.
- Cut 12 matching sets of 1 each 4½" x 5½" L rectangle and 2⅞" M square.

Tall House
6" x 16" Finished Block
Make 12

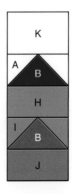

Short House
6" x 16" Finished Block
Make 12

Narrow House
4" x 16" Finished Block
Make 12

From assorted red batik scraps:

- Cut 20 (3½" x 7½") R strips, 18 (3½" x 6½") S strips and 4 (3½") T squares.
- Cut 9 (2¼" by fabric width) binding strips.
- Cut 12 (7¼") squares.
  Cut each square on both diagonals to make 48 B triangles.
- Cut 6 (5¼") squares.
  Cut each square on both diagonals to make 24 D triangles.

From white batik:

- Cut 1 (76½" by fabric width) strip.
  Subcut strip into 2 each 5½" x 76½" U, 5½" x 70½" V, 3½" x 64½" P and 3½" x 54½" Q strips.
- Cut 3 (3⅞" by fabric width) strips.
  Subcut strips into 24 (3⅞") squares. Cut each square in half on 1 diagonal to make 48 A triangles.
- Cut 1 (2⅞" by fabric width) strip.
  Subcut strip into 12 (2⅞") squares. Cut each square in half on 1 diagonal to make 24 C triangles.
- Cut 3 (4½" by fabric width) strips.
  Subcut strips into 12 each (4½" x 6½") K and (2½" x 4½") O rectangles.

Completing the Blocks

1. Sew an A triangle on one short side of a B triangle as shown in Figure 1a; press. Sew an A triangle on the remaining short side of B (Figure 1b) to make an A-B unit; press. Repeat to make a total of 24 A-B units.

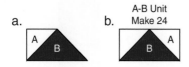

Figure 1

2. Sew a C triangle on one short side of a D triangle as shown in Figure 2a; press. Sew a C triangle on the remaining short side of D (Figure 2b) to make a C-D unit; press. Repeat to make a total of 12 C-D units.

Figure 2

Tall House Blocks

1. Select one each A-B unit, B triangle and G rectangle, and one matching set of one each E rectangle and F square for one block.

2. Cut the F square in half on one diagonal to make two F triangles. Sew the F triangles to the two short sides of the B triangle to make the B-F unit as shown in Figure 3; press.

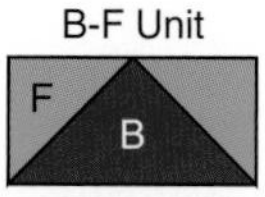

Figure 3

3. Arrange and join the units and the E and G rectangles in a vertical row referring to the block drawing to complete one Tall House block; press toward the rectangles.

4. Repeat steps 1–3 to make a total of 12 Tall House blocks.

Short House Blocks

1. Select one each A-B unit, B triangle and J and K rectangle, and one matching set of one each H rectangle and I square for one block.

2. Cut the I square in half on one diagonal to make two I triangles. Sew the I triangles to the two short sides of the B triangle to make the B-I unit as shown in Figure 4; press.

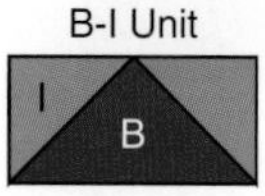

Figure 4

3. Arrange and join the units and the H, J and K rectangles in a vertical row referring to the block drawing to make one Short House block; press toward the rectangles.

4. Repeat steps 1–3 to make a total of 12 Short House blocks.

Narrow House Blocks

1. Select one each C-D unit, D triangle, N square and O rectangle, and one matching set of one each L rectangle and M square.

2. Cut the M square in half on one diagonal to make two M triangles. Sew the M triangles to the two short sides of the D triangle to make the D-M unit as shown in Figure 5; press.

D-M Unit

Figure 5

3. Arrange and join the units, N square, and L and O rectangles in a vertical row referring to the block drawing to make one Narrow House block; press away from the C-D and D-M units.

4. Repeat steps 1–3 to make a total of 12 Narrow House blocks.

Completing the Quilt

Refer to the Assembly Diagram for positioning of blocks and borders.

1. Arrange and sew three each Tall House, Short House and Narrow House blocks to make a row; press. Repeat to make a total of four rows.

2. Join the rows to complete the quilt center; press.

3. Sew P strips to opposite sides and Q strips to top and bottom of quilt center; press.

4. Sew 10 R strips together on short ends to make one side border strip; press. Repeat to make a second side border strip. Sew the strips to opposite sides of the quilt center; press.

5. Sew nine S strips together on short ends to make a long strip; press. Sew a T square to each end to make the top border strip; press. Repeat to make the bottom border strip. Sew the strips to the top and bottom of the quilt center; press.

6. Sew U strips to opposite sides of quilt center and V strips top and bottom to complete the quilt top; press.

7. Layer, quilt and bind referring to Quilting Basics on page 45. ●

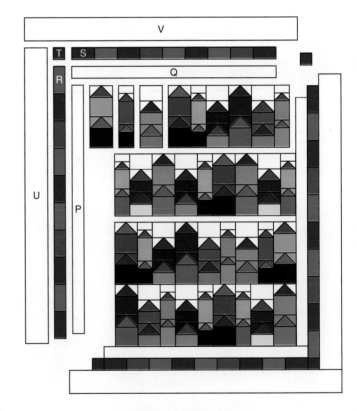

Village by the Sea
Assembly Diagram 70" x 86"

The Whole Box of Crayons

Scrappy doesn't mean messy—it means playing with unlimited colors.

Design by Chris Malone
Quilted by Jean McDaniel

Skill Level
Beginner

Specifications
Quilt Size: 63" x 63"
Block Size: 9" x 9" finished
Number of Blocks: 49

Materials
- ⅝ yard black print
- ⅝ yard white tonal
- 4¼ yards total assorted-color scraps
- Backing to size
- Batting to size
- Thread
- Basic sewing tools and supplies

Here's a Tip

"Often we worry about what colors 'go together,' but if you open up a big new box of crayons, all you see are bright, happy colors, each with its own personality. So use the whole box for the fullest experience!"

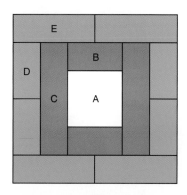

Crayons
9" x 9" Finished Block
Make 49

Project Notes
Read all instructions before beginning this project.

Stitch right sides together using a ¼" seam allowance unless otherwise specified.

Materials and cutting lists assume 40" of usable fabric width for yardage.

Cutting

From black print:
- Cut 7 (2¼" by fabric width) binding strips.

From white tonal:
- Cut 5 (3½" by fabric width) strips.
  Subcut strips into 49 (3½") A squares.

From assorted-color scraps:
- Cut 49 sets of 2 each matching-color 2" x 3½" B rectangles and 2" x 6½" C rectangles.
- Cut 49 sets of 4 each matching-color 2" x 3½" D rectangles and 2" x 5" E rectangles.

Completing the Blocks

1. For one block, select one matching-color set of B and C rectangles and a different-color set of D and E rectangles.

2. Sew B rectangles to opposite sides of an A square as shown in Figure 1 to make an A-B unit; press.

A-B Unit

Figure 1

3. Referring to Figure 2, sew C rectangles to opposite sides of A-B unit to complete block center; press.

Block Center

Figure 2

4. Sew two D rectangles together on short ends to make a D-D strip as shown in Figure 3; press. Repeat to make a second D-D strip. Repeat to make two E-E strips.

D-D Strip
Make 2

E-E Strip
Make 2

Figure 3

5. Sew D-D strips to opposite sides of block center; press. Sew E-E strips to top and bottom to complete one Crayons block; press.

6. Repeat steps 1–5 to make a total of 49 Crayons blocks.

Completing the Quilt

Refer to the Assembly Diagram for positioning of blocks.

1. Arrange and sew Crayons blocks into seven rows of seven blocks each turning every other block in each row; press.

2. Sew rows together to complete the quilt top; press.

3. Layer, quilt and bind referring to Quilting Basics on page 45. ●

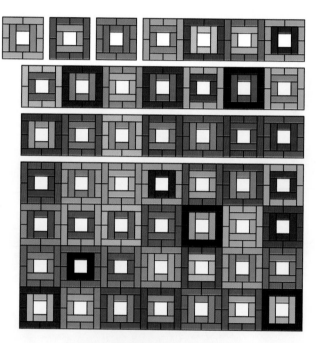

The Whole Box of Crayons
Assembly Diagram 63" x 63"

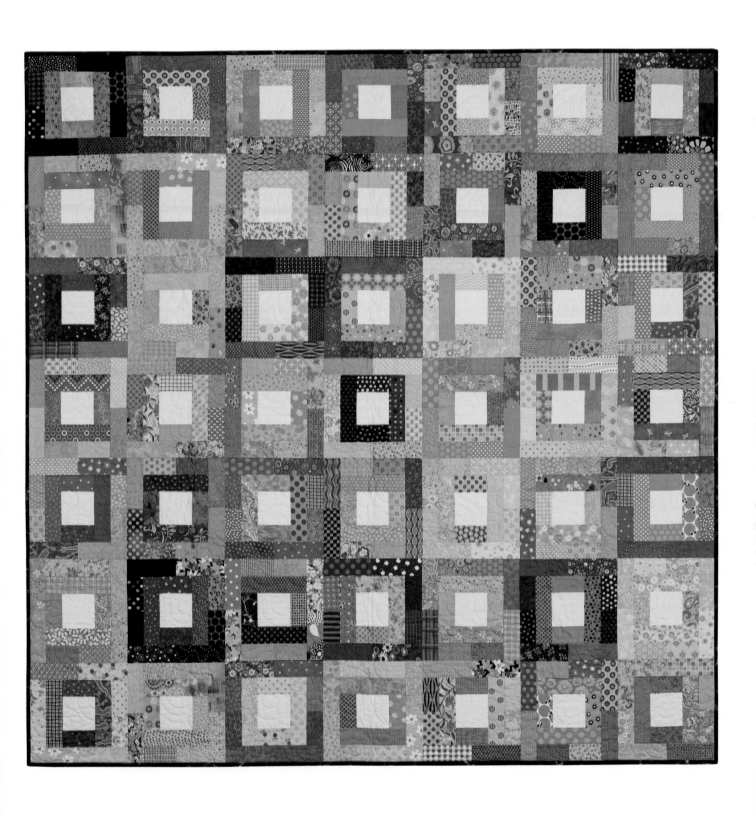

Color Perfect

If the scrappy look isn't your style, try coordinating the colors and use a solid background to bring it all together.

Designed & Quilted by Holly Daniels

Skill Level
Confident Beginner

Specifications
Quilt Size: 60" x 60"
Block Size: 15" x 15" finished
Number of Blocks: 16

Materials
- 2½ yards total green scraps
- ⅓ yard dark green tonal
- 3¼ yards white solid
- Backing to size
- Batting to size
- Thread
- Basic sewing tools and supplies

Project Notes
Read all instructions before beginning this project.

Stitch right sides together using a ¼" seam allowance unless otherwise specified.

Materials and cutting lists assume 40" of usable fabric width for yardage.

Cutting

From green scraps:
- Cut 2½" by various length strips to total 260" when joined for binding.
- Cut 128 (3⅞") B squares.

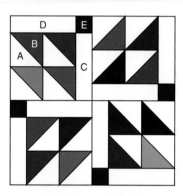

Color Perfect
15" x 15" Finished Block
Make 16

From dark green tonal:
- Cut 4 (2" by fabric width) E strips.

From white solid:
- Cut 13 (3⅞" by fabric width) strips.
  Subcut strips into 128 (3⅞") A squares.
- Cut 8 (6½" by fabric width) strips.
  Subcut 4 strips into 64 (2" x 6½") C strips.
  Label 4 remaining strips as D.

Completing the Block
1. Draw a diagonal line on the wrong side of each A square. Referring to Figure 1, pair A and B squares with right sides together and stitch ¼" from each side of drawn line. Cut on line to make two A-B units; press. Repeat to make a total of 256 A-B units.

Figure 1

2. Arrange and stitch four A-B units into two rows as shown in Figure 2a; press. Referring to Figure 2b, sew rows together to make a corner unit; press. Repeat to make a total of 64 corner units.

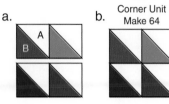

Figure 2

3. Sew one each E and D strip on long sides to make a strip set as shown in Figure 3; press seam toward E. Repeat to make a total of four strip sets. Subcut strip sets into 64 (2" x 8") D-E units.

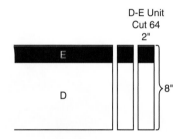

Figure 3

4. Referring to Figure 4, stitch a C strip to one side of each corner unit; press.

Figure 4

5. Stitch a D-E unit onto the adjacent side of each corner unit as shown in Figure 5 to make 64 quarter blocks; press.

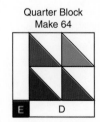

Figure 5

6. Arrange four quarter blocks as shown in the block drawing. Stitch quarter blocks into rows, then join rows to complete one Color Perfect block; press seams toward white sides to reduce bulk. Repeat to make a total of 16 blocks.

Completing the Quilt
Refer to the Assembly Diagram for positioning of blocks.

1. Arrange and sew blocks into four rows of four blocks each; press.

2. Sew rows together to complete the quilt top; press.

3. Layer, quilt and bind referring to Quilting Basics on page 45. ●

Color Perfect
Assembly Diagram 60" x 60"

Scrap Basket Table Runner

Turn your scraps and stash into something beautiful.
Sort your favorite dark neutrals for the baskets
and add touches of color to fill those baskets.

Designed & Quilted by Chris Malone

Skill Level

Confident Beginner

Specifications

Runner Size: 48" x 16"
Block Size: 8" x 8" finished
Number of Blocks: 12

Materials

- Scrap black solid
- Scraps 12 bright florals
- ⅜ yard multicolored print
- ½ yard total assorted gray and black scraps
- ¾ yard white-with-black dots
- Backing to size
- Batting to size
- 2 (1"-diameter) black buttons
- Thread
- Basic sewing tools and supplies

Project Notes

Read all instructions before beginning this project.

Stitch right sides together using a ¼" seam allowance unless otherwise specified.

Materials and cutting lists assume 40" of usable fabric width for yardage.

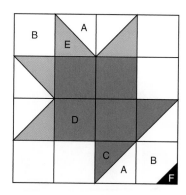

Basket
8" x 8" Finished Block
Make 12

Cutting

From black solid scrap:

- Cut 12 (1½") F squares.

From each bright floral scrap:

- Cut 2 (2⅞") E squares.

From multicolored print:

- Cut 4 (2¼" by fabric width) binding strips.

From assorted gray & black scraps:

- Cut 12 matching sets of 1 (2⅞") C square and 4 (2½") D squares.

From white-with-black dots:

- Cut 3 (2⅞" by fabric width) strips.
  Subcut strips into 36 (2⅞") A squares.
- Cut 5 (2½" by fabric width) strips.
  Subcut strips into 72 (2½") B squares.

Completing the Block

1. Draw a diagonal line on the wrong side of each A and F square.

2. Select three A squares, six B squares, one set of C and D squares, two same-floral E squares and one F square for one Basket block.

3. Referring to Figure 1, pair A and C squares with right sides together and stitch ¼" from each side of drawn line. Cut on line to make two A-C units; press.

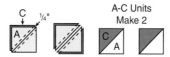

Figure 1

4. Pair A and E squares with right sides together and stitch ¼" from each side of drawn line as shown in Figure 2. Cut on line to make two A-E units; press. Repeat to make a total of four A-E units.

Figure 2

5. Referring to Figure 3, place an F square right sides together on one corner of a B square and stitch on the drawn line. Trim the seam to ¼" and press open to make a B-F unit.

Figure 3

6. Arrange and stitch A-C, A-E and B-F units and B and D squares into rows referring to Figure 4; press. Sew rows together to complete one Basket block; press.

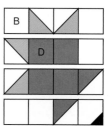

Figure 4

7. Repeat steps 2–6 to make a total of 12 Basket blocks.

Completing the Quilt

1. Arrange four Basket blocks with black F triangles meeting in the center as shown in Figure 5. Sew blocks into two rows and stitch rows together to make a four-basket section. Repeat to make a total of three four-basket sections.

Four-Basket Section
Make 3

Figure 5

2. Sew the three sections together to complete the runner top referring to the Assembly Diagram; press.

3. Layer, quilt and bind referring to Quilting Basics on page 45.

4. Hand-sew a black button to the center of the background space between each four-basket section to finish. ●

Scrap Basket Table Runner
Assembly Diagram 48" x 16"

Cakes

Celebrate your stash and scraps with some Cake blocks.
What better way to use luscious fabrics than in a super-sweet treat!

Designed & Quilted by Tricia Lynn Maloney

Skill Level
Confident Beginner

Specifications
Quilt Size: 50" x 50"
Block Size: 10" x 10" finished
Number of Blocks: 16

Materials
- 16 precut 2½"-wide assorted scrap strips
- ⅝ yard red solid
- 1⅞ yards white solid
- Backing to size
- Batting to size
- Thread
- Basic sewing tools and supplies

Project Notes
Read all instructions before beginning this project.

Stitch right sides together using a ¼" seam allowance unless otherwise specified.

Materials and cutting lists assume 40" of usable fabric width for yardage.

Cutting

From precut scrap strips:
- Cut 16 each 2½" A squares, 2½" x 4½" B strips, 2½" x 6½" C strips, 2½" x 8½" D strips and 2½" x 10½" E strips.

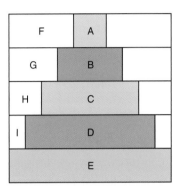

Cake
10" x 10" Finished Block
Make 16

From red solid:
- Cut 1 (2½" by fabric width) strip.
  Subcut strip into 13 (2½") K squares.
- Cut 6 (2¼" by fabric width) binding strips.

From white solid:
- Cut 17 (2½" by fabric width) strips.
  Subcut strips into 24 (2½" x 10½") J strips, and 32 each 2½" H squares, 2½" x 1½" I rectangles, 2½" x 3½" G rectangles and 2½" x 4½" F rectangles.
- Cut 5 (2½" by fabric width) L strips.

Completing the Blocks
1. Sew F rectangles on each end of an A square as shown in Figure 1 to make an A-F unit; press. Repeat to make 16 A-F units.

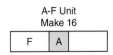

A-F Unit
Make 16

Figure 1

2. Referring to Figure 2, sew G rectangles to each end of a B strip to make a B-G unit; press. Repeat to make 16 B-G units.

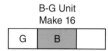

B-G Unit
Make 16

Figure 2

3. Sew H squares on each end of a C strip as shown in Figure 3 to make a C-H unit; press. Repeat to make 16 C-H units.

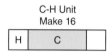

C-H Unit
Make 16

Figure 3

4. Referring to Figure 4, sew I rectangles to each end of a D strip to make a D-I unit; press. Repeat to make 16 D-I units.

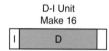

D-I Unit
Make 16

Figure 4

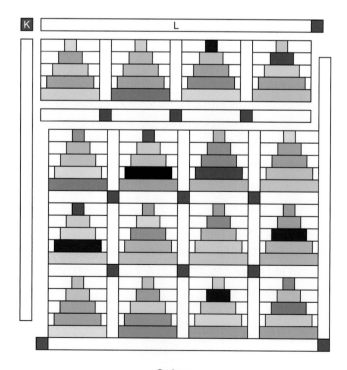

Cakes
Assembly Diagram 50" x 50"

5. Arrange and stitch together one each A-F, B-G, C-H and D-I unit with an E rectangle as shown in Figure 5 to complete one Cake block; press.

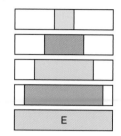

Figure 5

6. Repeat step 5 to make a total of 16 Cake blocks.

Completing the Quilt

Refer to the Assembly Diagram for positioning of block and sashing rows.

1. Arrange and sew four blocks and three J strips into a block row as shown in Figure 6; press. Repeat to make a total of four block rows.

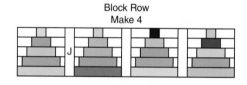

Block Row
Make 4

Figure 6

2. Referring to Figure 7, arrange and sew four J strips and three K squares into a sashing row; press. Repeat to make a total of three sashing rows.

Sashing Row
Make 3

Figure 7

3. Alternately sew block and sashing rows together to complete the quilt center; press.

4. Sew L strips together on the short ends to make one long strip; press. Subcut strip into four 2½" x 46½" L strips.

5. Sew L strips to opposite sides of quilt center, press.

6. Sew K squares on opposite ends of remaining L strips to make two K-L border units; press.

7. Sew K-L border units to top and bottom of quilt center to complete the quilt top; press.

8. Layer, quilt and bind referring to Quilting Basics on page 45. ●

Checks & Balances

This timeless pattern will eat up those small pieces of favorite fabrics and showcase them at the same time.

Design by Bev Getschel
Quilted by Cindy Meservey

Skill Level
Intermediate

Specifications
Quilt Size: 78" x 92"
Block Size: 12" x 12" finished
Number of Blocks: 24

Materials
- 120 pastel batik scraps at least 1½" x 20"
- 1½ yards navy blue 2 batik
- 2¼ yards navy blue 1 batik
- 4½ yards light blue batik
- Backing to size
- Batting to size
- Thread
- Basic sewing tools and supplies

Project Notes
Read all instructions before beginning this project.

Stitch right sides together using a ¼" seam allowance unless otherwise specified.

Materials and cutting lists assume 40" of usable fabric width for yardage.

Cutting

From pastel batik scraps:
- Cut 120 (1½" x 20") A strips.

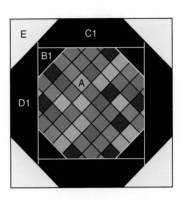

Octagon 1
12" x 12" Finished Block
Make 10

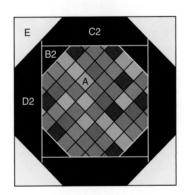

Octagon 2
12" x 12" Finished Block
Make 14

From navy blue 2 batik:
- Cut 3 (3¼" by fabric width) strips.
  Subcut strips into 28 (3¼") squares. Cut each square in half on 1 diagonal to make 56 B2 triangles.
- Cut 2 (8½" by fabric width) strips.
  Subcut strips into 28 (2½" x 8½") C2 strips.
- Cut 2 (9½" by fabric width) strips.
  Subcut strips into 28 (2½" x 9½") D2 strips.

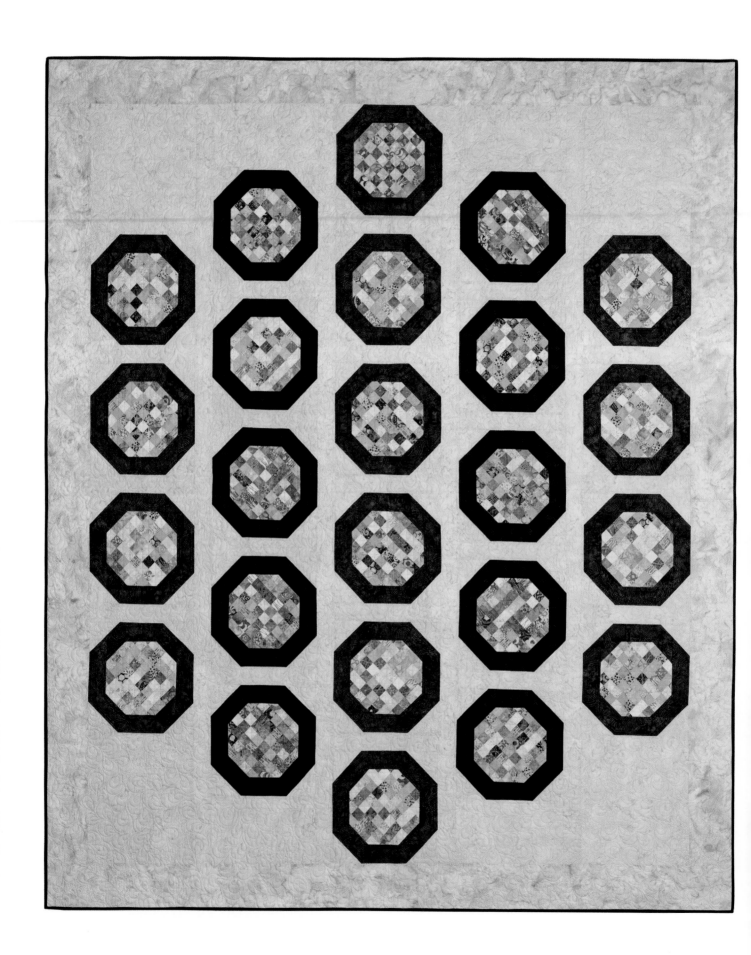

Stash-Busting Quilts

From navy blue 1 batik:

- Cut 2 (3¼" by fabric width) strips.
  Subcut strips into 20 (3¼") squares. Cut each
  square in half on 1 diagonal to make 40
  B1 triangles.
- Cut 2 (8½" by fabric width) strips.
  Subcut strips into 20 (2½" x 8½") C1 strips.
- Cut 2 (9½" by fabric width) strips.
  Subcut strips into 20 (2½" x 9½") D1 strips.
- Cut 9 (2¼" by fabric width) binding strips.

From light blue batik:

- Cut 6 (4⅜" by fabric width) strips.
  Subcut strips into 48 (4⅜") squares. Cut each
  square in half on 1 diagonal to make
  96 E triangles.
- Cut 4 (12½" by fabric width) strips.
  Subcut strips into 19 (2½" x 12½") F strips,
  4 (12½" x 14½") G rectangles and 4 (7½" x 12½")
  H rectangles.
- Cut 9 (2½" by fabric width) I strips.
- Cut 9 (5½" by fabric width) J/K strips.

Completing the Blocks

1. Sew eight A strips together lengthwise to make
a strip set as shown in Figure 1; press. Repeat to
make a total of 15 strip sets. Subcut strip sets into
192 (1½" x 8½") A segments.

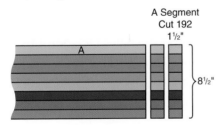

A Segment
Cut 192
1½"

A

8½"

Figure 1

2. Referring to Figure 2, arrange and stitch eight A
segments together to make an A unit; press. Repeat
to make 24 A units.

A Unit
Make 24

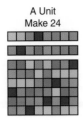

Figure 2

3. To make an Octagon 1 block, select one A unit,
four B1 triangles and two each C1 and D1 strips.

4. Center and stitch B1 triangles to opposite sides
of an A unit as shown in Figure 3a; press. Sew B1
triangles to remaining sides referring to Figure 3b;
press. Rotate unit so A unit is on-point and trim to
8½" square to make checkerboard unit as shown in
Figures 3c and 3d.

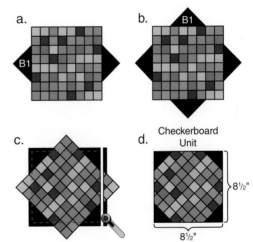

a.

B1

B1

b.

B1

c.

d.

Checkerboard
Unit

8½"

8½"

Figure 3

5. Referring to Figure 4, sew C strips to top and
bottom of checkerboard unit; press. Center and
sew D strips to opposite sides of checkerboard
unit; press.

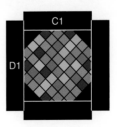

C1

D1

Figure 4

6. Using a ruler and rotary cutter, trim corners 2¼" from A-B seam as shown in Figure 5. Trim remaining corners to make an octagon.

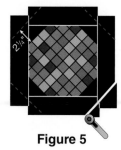

Figure 5

7. Referring to Figure 6, sew E triangles to each corner to complete one Octagon 1 block; press. Trim block to 12½" square, if necessary.

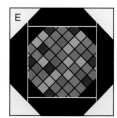

Figure 6

8. Repeat steps 3–7 to make a total of 10 Octagon 1 blocks.

9. Repeat steps 4–7 to make 14 Octagon 2 blocks using one A unit, four B2 triangles, and two each C2 and D2 strips for each block.

Completing the Quilt

Refer to the Assembly Diagram for positioning of rows, strips and borders.

1. Arrange and join four Octagon 2 blocks, two G rectangles and three F strips as shown in Figure 7 to make Row A; press. Repeat to make a second Row A.

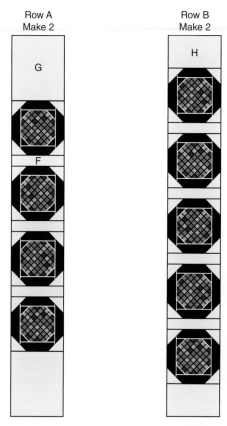

Figure 7   **Figure 8**

2. Arrange and stitch five Octagon 1 blocks, two H rectangles and four F strips as shown in Figure 8 to make Row B; press. Repeat to make a second Row B.

3. Arrange and alternately sew six Octagon 2 blocks and five F strips as shown in Figure 9 to make Row C; press.

Row C
Make 1

Figure 9

4. Sew I strips together on short ends to make one long strip. Subcut strip into four 2½" x 82½" I strips.

5. Sew Rows A–C and I strips together to complete the quilt center; press.

6. Sew J/K strips together on short ends to make one long strip. Subcut strip into two each 5½" x 82½" J and 5½" x 78½" K strips.

7. Sew J strips to opposite sides of quilt center and K strips to the top and bottom to complete the quilt top; press.

8. Layer, quilt and bind referring to Quilting Basics on page 45. ●

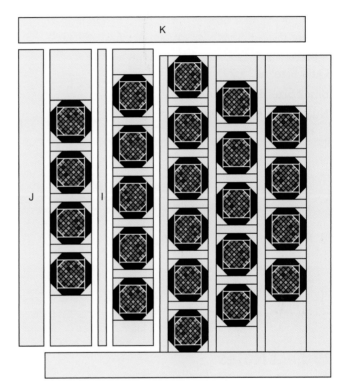

Checks & Balances
Assembly Diagram 78" x 92"

Nose-Diving Quilt

This is the perfect quilt to use all those leftover 2½" strips or, if need be, cut the colors from your stash.

Design by Nancy Scott
Quilted by Masterpiece Quilting

Skill Level
Confident Beginner

Specifications
Quilt Size: 60" x 72"
Block Size: 12" x 6" finished
Number of Blocks: 60

Materials
- 55–60 precut 2½" assorted scrap strips
- 2⅔ yards neutral solid
- Backing to size
- Batting to size
- Thread
- Ruler with 45-degree line
- Basic sewing tools and supplies

Project Notes
Read all instructions before beginning this project.

Stitch right sides together using a ¼" seam allowance unless otherwise specified.

Materials and cutting lists assume 40" of usable fabric width for yardage.

Cutting

From precut scrap strips:
- Cut 16 (2½" x 20") binding strips.
- Cut 60 each 2½" x 5½" A strips, 2½" x 9½" B strips and 2½" x 13½" C strips.

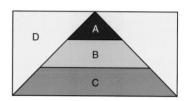

Flying Geese
12" x 6" Finished Block
Make 60

From neutral solid:
- Cut 12 (6⅞" by fabric width) strips.
  Subcut strips into 60 (6⅞") squares. Cut each square in half on 1 diagonal to make 120 D triangles.

Completing the Blocks

1. Center and sew one each A, B and C strip together on the long sides as shown in Figure 1 to make a strip set; press. Fold in half top to bottom and press lightly to mark centerline.

Figure 1

2. Referring to Figure 2, align the 45-degree line of ruler 6⅝" from bottom centerline and ⅛" from top center of strip set and, using a rotary cutter, trim excess fabric from one end. Repeat on opposite end to make a triangle.

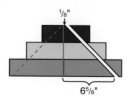

Figure 2

3. Sew D triangles to the angled sides of A-B-C triangle referring to the block drawing to complete one Flying Geese block; press.

4. Repeat steps 1–3 to make a total of 60 Flying Geese blocks.

Completing the Quilt

Refer to the Assembly Diagram for positioning of blocks.

1. Arrange and sew Flying Geese blocks into 12 rows; press.

2. Sew rows together to complete the quilt top; press.

3. Layer, quilt and bind referring to Quilting Basics on page 45. ●

Nose-Diving Quilt
Assembly Diagram 60" x 72"

Simply Sophisticated Table Runner

Think about the kinds of fabrics in your scraps and stash; even scraps can be themed. Fabrics come in every theme from patriotic to holiday.

Design by Nancy Scott
Quilted by Masterpiece Quilting

Skill Level
Confident Beginner

Specifications
Quilt Size: 75" x 19"
Block Size: 15" x 15" finished
Number of Blocks: 4

Materials
- Scraps of 4 different blue tonals
- Scraps of 4 different red tonals
- ⅔ yard cream tonal
- 1¼ yards dark blue dot
- Backing to size
- Batting to size
- Thread
- Basic sewing tools and supplies

Project Notes
Read all instructions before beginning this project.

Stitch right sides together using a ¼" seam allowance unless otherwise specified.

Materials and cutting lists assume 40" of usable fabric width for yardage.

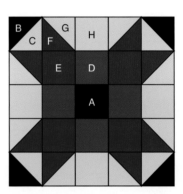

Four X Star
15" x 15" Finished Block
Make 4

Cutting

From each blue tonal scrap:
- Cut 4 (3½") D squares.

From each red tonal scrap:
- Cut 4 each 3½" E squares and 3⅞" F squares.

From cream tonal:
- Cut 1 (7¼" by fabric width) strip.
    Subcut strip into 1 (7¼") square. Cut in half on 1 diagonal to make 2 I triangles.
- Cut remainder of 7¼" strip into 2 (3½" by remaining fabric width) strips.
    Subcut strips into 16 (3½") H squares.
- Cut 3 (3⅞" by fabric width) strips.
    Subcut strips into 8 (3⅞") C squares and 16 (3⅞") G squares.

From dark blue dot:

- Cut 5 (2¼" by fabric width) binding strips.
- Cut 1 (3½" by fabric width) strip.
  Subcut strip into 4 (3½") A squares.
- Cut 1 (3⅞" by fabric width) strip.
  Subcut strip into 8 (3⅞") B squares.
- Cut 2 (2⅝" by fabric width) strips.
  Subcut strips into 2 each 2⅝" x 10" J strips
    and 2⅝" x 12" K strips.
- Cut 4 (2½" by fabric width) L strips.

Completing the Blocks

1. Draw a diagonal line on the wrong side of each C and G square.

2. Referring to Figure 1, pair C and B squares with right sides together and stitch ¼" from each side of drawn line. Cut on line to make two B-C units; press. Repeat to make a total of 16 B-C units.

Figure 1

3. Pair G and F squares with right sides together and stitch ¼" from each side of drawn line as shown in Figure 2. Cut on line to make two F-G units; press. Repeat to make a total of 32 F-G units.

Figure 2

4. To make one block, select eight same-fabric F-G units and four matching E squares, four same-fabric D squares, four B-C units, one A square and four H squares.

5. Arrange and stitch units and squares into rows referring to Figure 3; press. Sew rows together to complete one Four X Star block; press.

Figure 3

6. Repeat steps 4 and 5 to make a total of four blocks.

Completing the End Triangles

1. Sew a J strip to one short side of an I triangle as shown in Figure 4; press.

Figure 4

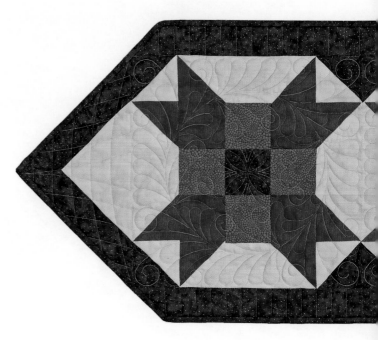

2. Referring to Figure 5a, sew a K strip to the adjacent short side of I; press. Trim ends of J and K strips even with the long edge of I to make one end triangle 5b.

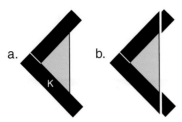

a. b.

K

Figure 5

3. Repeat steps 1 and 2 to make a second end triangle.

Completing the Table Runner

Refer to the Assembly Diagram and project photo throughout for positioning of blocks, end triangles and border.

1. Sew blocks together to form a row; press.

2. Sew end triangles on opposite ends of row; press.

3. Sew L strips together on short ends to make one long strip. Subcut strip into two 2½" x 62" L strips.

4. Center and sew L strips to opposite long sides of pieced center. Trim ends of L strips even with angled edges of end triangles to complete the table runner top; press.

5. Layer, quilt and bind referring to Quilting Basics on page 45. ●

Here's a Tip

To custom-fit the length of the table runner to your table, simply change the number of blocks.

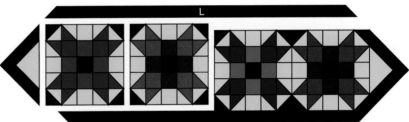

L

Simply Sophisticated Table Runner
Assembly Diagram 75" x 19"

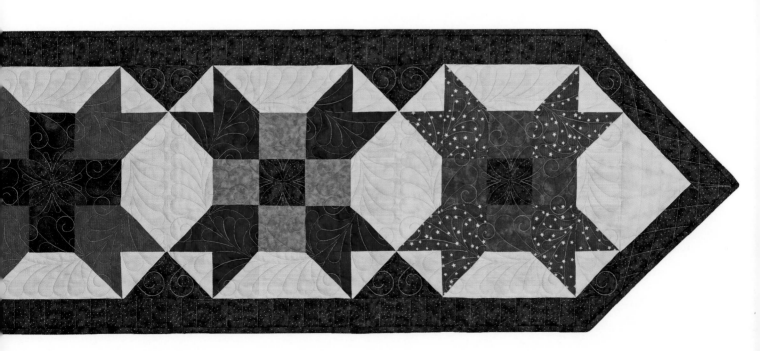

Welcome to the Neighborhood

Create your own neighborhood and personalize it with your chosen colors with this great scrap buster!

Designed & Quilted by Lolita Newman

Skill Level

Intermediate

Specifications

Quilt Size: 80" x 80"
Block Size: 8" x 8" finished
Number of Blocks: 96

Here's a Tip

For a super-scrappy look, incorporate lots of different fabrics into the quilt. For a more uniform look, use fabrics that are very similar in color and print.

Materials

- 33 light and dark 9" x 10" scraps for houses
- ⅝ yard white tonal
- ⅞ yard brick print
- 1⅛ yards green tonal
- 1¼ yards total assorted yellow scraps
- 1½ yards total assorted light scraps
- 1⅔ yards total assorted dark scraps
- 1¾ yards taupe tonal
- Backing to size
- Batting to size
- Thread
- Template material
- Basic sewing tools and supplies

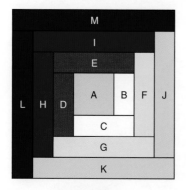

Log Cabin
8" x 8" Finished Block
Make 32

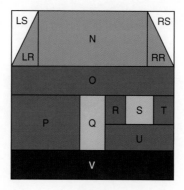

House 1
8" x 8" Finished Block
Make 63

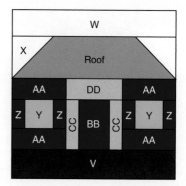

House 2
8" x 8" Finished Block
Make 1

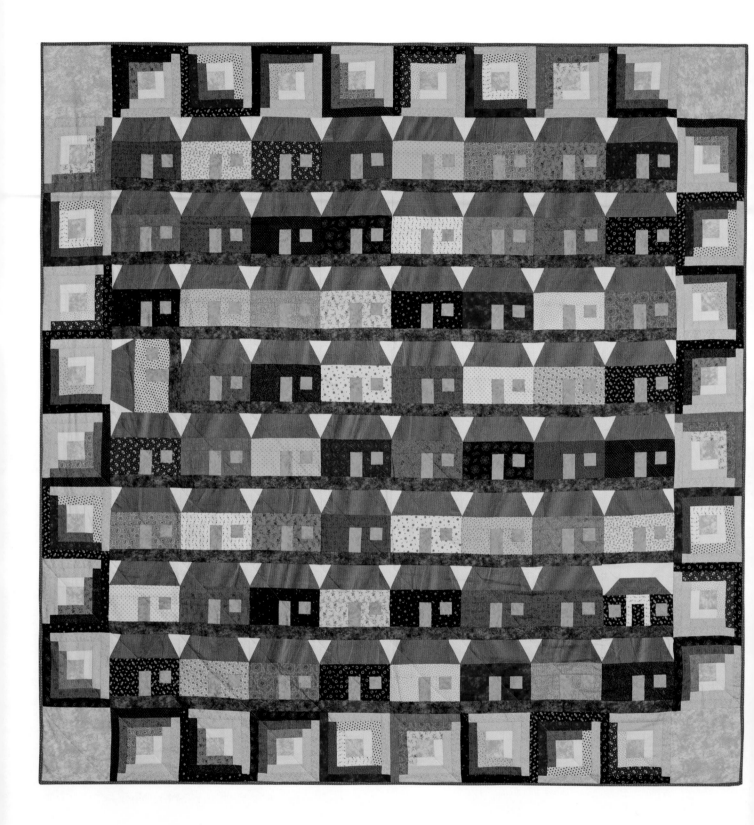

Project Notes

Read all instructions before beginning this project.

Stitch right sides together using a ¼" seam allowance unless otherwise specified.

Materials and cutting lists assume 40" of usable fabric width for yardage.

Cutting

Prepare templates using full-size patterns given.

From 1 dark house scrap:

- Cut 1 each 1⅞" x 8½" O, 3⅛" x 3⅞" P, 1½" x 1⅞" R, 1½" x 1⅞" T and 1¾" x 3⅞" U rectangle.
- Cut 4 each 1⅛" x 1⅞" Z and 1½" x 3⅛" AA rectangles.
- Cut 1 (2" x 2⅞") BB rectangle.

From 1 light house scrap:

- Cut 2 (1⅛" x 2⅞") CC and 1 (1½" x 3¼") DD rectangles.

From each of 31 remaining house scraps:

- Cut 2 each 1⅞" x 8½" O, 3⅛" x 3⅞" P, 1½" x 1⅞" R, 1½" x 1⅞" T and 1¾" x 3⅞" U rectangles.

From white tonal:

- Cut 1 (1¾" x 8½") W rectangle and 1 (2⅞") square. Cut square in half on 1 diagonal to make 2 X triangles.
- Using templates, cut 63 each right (RS) and left (LS) sky triangles.

From brick print:

- Cut 9 (2¼" by fabric width) binding strips.

From green tonal:

- Cut 4 (8½" by fabric width) strips. Subcut strips into 64 (1⅞" x 8½") V rectangles.

From assorted yellow scraps:

- Cut 32 (2½") A squares, 4 (8½") EE squares, 63 (1⅞") S squares, 63 (1¾" x 3⅛") Q rectangles and 2 (1⅞") Y squares.

From assorted light scraps:

- Cut 32 pairs of matching 1½" x 7½" K and 1½" x 6½" J rectangles.
- Cut 32 pairs of matching 1½" x 5½" G and 1½" x 4½" F rectangles.
- Cut 32 pairs of matching 1½" x 3½" C and 1½" x 2½" B rectangles.

From assorted dark scraps:

- Cut 32 pairs of matching 1½" x 8½" M and 1½" x 7½" L rectangles.
- Cut 32 pairs of matching 1½" x 6½" I and 1½" x 5½" H rectangles.
- Cut 32 pairs of matching 1½" x 4½" E and 1½" x 3½" D rectangles.

From taupe tonal:

- Cut 6 (5⅞" by fabric width) strips. Subcut strips into 63 (3⅛" x 5⅞") N rectangles.
- Using right and left roof edge templates, cut 63 each RR right roof triangles and LR left roof triangles.
- Using roof template, cut 1 roof piece.

Completing the Blocks

Log Cabin Blocks

1. Select matching B and C rectangles. Stitch B rectangle to one side of an A square as shown in Figure 1a; press. Stitch a C rectangle to the adjacent side of the A-B unit referring to Figure 1b; press.

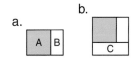

Figure 1

2. Select matching D and E rectangles. Referring to Figure 2a, stitch D to the adjacent side of the pieced unit; press. Stitch E to the next side of the pieced unit; press.

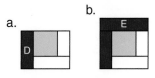

Figure 2

3. Select matching F and G, and matching H and I rectangles. Continue stitching rectangles in a clockwise order onto the pieced unit as shown in Figure 3, pressing after each seam.

Figure 3

4. Select matching J and K and matching L and M rectangles. Referring to Figure 4, continue stitching rectangles in a clockwise order onto the pieced unit to complete one Log Cabin block, pressing after each seam.

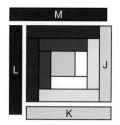

Figure 4

5. Repeat steps 1–4 to complete a total of 32 Log Cabin blocks.

House 1 Blocks

1. Select one each LS, RS, LR and RR triangles. Stitch LS to LR on long sides to make the left roof unit as shown in Figure 5; press. Repeat with RS and RR to make the right roof unit.

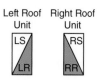

Figure 5

2. Referring to Figure 6, arrange and stitch roof units on opposite ends of an N rectangle to make the roof unit; press.

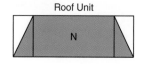

Figure 6

3. Select matching O, P, R, T and U pieces. Sew R and T rectangles to opposite sides of an S square as shown in Figure 7, press.

Figure 7

4. Referring to Figure 8, sew a U rectangle to the bottom of the R-S-T unit to make the window unit; press.

Figure 8

5. Sew P and Q rectangles to the window unit as shown in Figure 9 to make the house center unit; press.

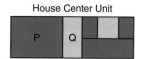

Figure 9

6. Referring to Figure 10, arrange and join the roof unit, O rectangle, house center unit and V rectangle to complete one House 1 block; press.

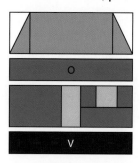

Figure 10

7. Repeat steps 1–6 to make a total of 63 House 1 blocks.

House 2 Block

1. Sew X triangles to opposite ends of the roof piece as shown in Figure 11 to make the roof unit; press.

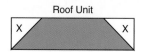

Figure 11

2. Referring to Figure 12a, stitch Z rectangles to opposite sides of Y square; press. Stitch AA strips to top and bottom of Y-Z unit to make a window unit as shown in Figure 12b; press. Repeat to make a second window unit.

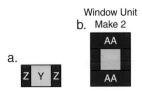

Figure 12

3. Referring to Figure 13a, stitch CC rectangles to opposite sides of BB; press. Stitch DD strip to top of BB-CC unit to make the door unit as shown in Figure 13b; press.

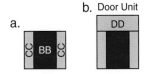

Figure 13

4. Arrange and stitch window units on opposite sides of door unit to make the house center unit; press.

5. Referring to Figure 14, arrange and join the W rectangle, roof unit, house center unit and V rectangle to complete the House 2 block; press.

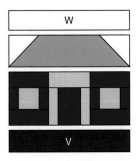

Figure 14

Completing the Quilt

Refer to the Assembly Diagram and project photo throughout for positioning of blocks.

1. Arrange and stitch EE squares and Log Cabin, House 1 and House 2 blocks together to form 10 rows; press.

2. Sew rows together to complete the quilt top; press.

3. Layer, quilt and bind referring to Quilting Basics on page 45. ●

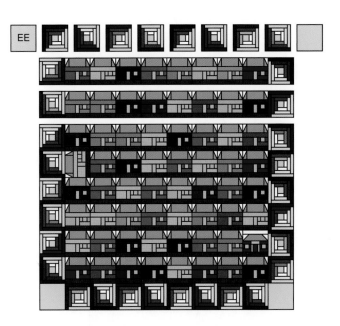

Welcome to the Neighborhood
Assembly Diagram 80" x 80"

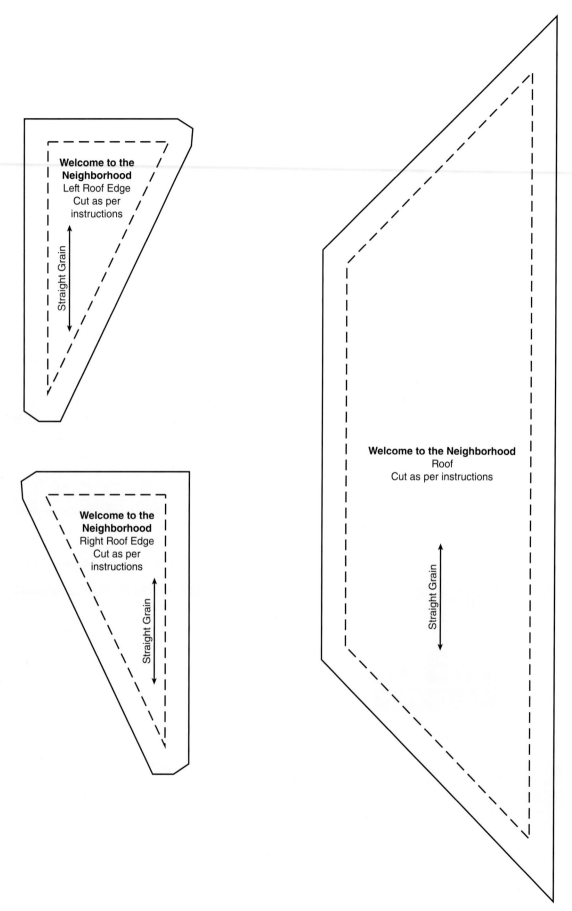

Welcome to the Neighborhood
Left Roof Edge
Cut as per
instructions

Straight Grain

Welcome to the Neighborhood
Right Roof Edge
Cut as per
instructions

Straight Grain

Welcome to the Neighborhood
Roof
Cut as per instructions

Straight Grain

Quilting Basics

The following is a reference guide. For more information, consult a comprehensive quilting book.

Always:

- Read through the entire pattern before you begin your project.
- Purchase quality, 100 percent cotton fabrics.
- When considering prewashing, do so with ALL of the fabrics being used. Generally, prewashing is not required in quilting.
- Use ¼" seam allowance for all stitching unless otherwise instructed.
- Use a short-to-medium stitch length.
- Make sure your seams are accurate.

Quilting Tools & Supplies

- Rotary cutter and mat
- Scissors for paper and fabric
- Non-slip quilting rulers
- Marking tools
- Sewing machine
- Sewing machine feet:
    - ¼" seaming foot (for piecing)
    - Walking or even-feed foot (for piecing or quilting)
    - Darning or free-motion foot (for free-motion quilting)
- Quilting hand-sewing needles
- Straight pins
- Curved safety pins for basting
- Seam ripper
- Iron and ironing surface

Basic Techniques

Appliqué

Fusible Appliqué

All templates are reversed for use with this technique.

1. Trace the instructed number of templates ¼" apart onto the paper side of paper-backed fusible web. Cut apart the templates, leaving a margin around each, and fuse to the wrong side of the fabric following fusible web manufacturer's instructions.

2. Cut the appliqué pieces out on the traced lines, remove paper backing and fuse to the background referring to the appliqué motif given.

3. Finish appliqué raw edges with a straight, satin, blanket, zigzag or blind-hem machine stitch with matching or invisible thread.

Turned-Edge Appliqué

1. Trace the printed reversed templates onto template plastic. Flip the template over and mark as the right side.

2. Position the template, right side up, on the right side of fabric and lightly trace, spacing images ½" apart. Cut apart, leaving a ¼" margin around the traced lines.

3. Clip curves and press edges ¼" to the wrong side around the appliqué shape.

4. Referring to the appliqué motif, pin or baste appliqué shapes to the background.

5. Hand-stitch shapes in place using a blind stitch and thread to match or machine-stitch using a short blind hemstitch and either matching or invisible thread.

Borders

Most patterns give an exact size to cut borders. You may check those sizes by comparing them to the horizontal and vertical center measurements of your quilt top.

Straight Borders

1. Mark the centers of the side borders and quilt top sides.

2. Stitch borders to quilt top sides with right sides together and matching raw edges and center marks using a ¼" seam. Press seams toward borders.

3. Repeat with top and bottom border lengths.

Mitered Borders

1. Add at least twice the border width to the border lengths instructed to cut.

2. Center and sew the side borders to the quilt, beginning and ending stitching ¼" from the quilt corner and backstitching (Figure 1). Repeat with the top and bottom borders.

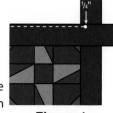

Figure 1

3. Fold and pin quilt right sides together at a 45-degree angle on one corner (Figure 2). Place a straightedge along the fold and lightly mark a line across the border ends.

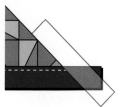

Figure 2

4. Stitch along the line, backstitching to secure. Trim seam to ¼" and press open (Figure 3).

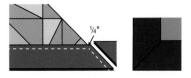

Figure 3

Quilt Backing & Batting

We suggest that you cut your backing and batting 8" larger than the finished quilt-top size. If preparing the backing from standard-width fabrics, remove the selvages and sew two or three lengths together; press seams open. If using 108"-wide fabric, trim to size on the straight grain of the fabric.

Prepare batting the same size as your backing. You can purchase prepackaged sizes or battings by the yard and trim to size.

Quilting

1. Press quilt top on both sides and trim all loose threads.

2. Make a quilt sandwich by layering the backing right side down, batting and quilt top centered right side up on flat surface and smooth out. Pin or baste layers together to hold.

3. Mark quilting design on quilt top and quilt as desired by hand or machine. *Note: If you are sending your quilt to a professional quilter, contact them for specifics about preparing your quilt for quilting.*

4. When quilting is complete, remove pins or basting. Trim batting and backing edges even with raw edges of quilt top.

Binding the Quilt

1. Join binding strips on short ends with diagonal seams to make one long strip; trim seams to ¼" and press seams open (Figure 4).

2. Fold 1" of one short end to wrong side and press. Fold the binding strip in half with wrong sides together along length, again referring to Figure 4; press.

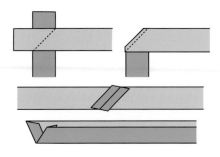

Figure 4

3. Starting about 3" from the folded short end, sew binding to quilt top edges, matching raw edges and using a ¼" seam. Stop stitching ¼" from corner and backstitch (Figure 5).

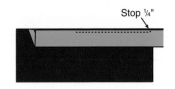

Figure 5

4. Fold binding up at a 45-degree angle to seam and then down even with quilt edges, forming a pleat at corner, referring to Figure 6.

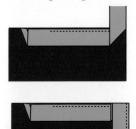

Figure 6

5. Resume stitching from corner edge as shown in Figure 6, down quilt side, backstitching ¼" from next corner. Repeat, mitering all corners, stitching to within 3" of starting point.

6. Trim binding end long enough to tuck inside starting end and complete stitching (Figure 7).

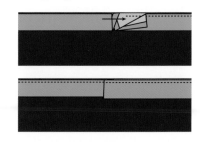

Figure 7

7. Fold binding to quilt back and stitch in place by hand or machine to complete your quilt.

Quilting Terms

- **Appliqué:** Adding fabric motifs to a foundation fabric by hand or machine (see Appliqué section of Basic Techniques).

- **Basting:** This temporarily secures layers of quilting materials together with safety pins, thread or a spray adhesive in preparation for quilting the layers.

  Use a long, straight stitch to hand- or machine-stitch one element to another holding the elements in place during construction and usually removed after construction.

- **Batting:** An insulating material made in a variety of fiber contents that is used between the quilt top and back to provide extra warmth and loft.

- **Binding:** A finishing strip of fabric sewn to the outer raw edges of a quilt to cover them.

  Straight-grain binding strips, cut on the crosswise straight grain of the fabric (see Straight & Bias Grain Lines illustration on page 47), are commonly used.

  Bias binding strips are cut at a 45-degree angle to the straight grain of the fabric. They are used when binding is being added to curved edges.

- **Block:** The basic quilting unit that is repeated to complete the quilt's design composition. Blocks can be pieced, appliquéd or solid and are usually square or rectangular in shape.
- **Border:** The frame of a quilt's central design used to visually complete the design and give the eye a place to rest.
- **Fabric Grain:** The fibers that run either parallel (lengthwise grain) or perpendicular (crosswise grain) to the fabric selvage are straight grain.

  Bias is any diagonal line between the lengthwise or crosswise grain. At these angles the fabric is less stable and stretches easily. The true bias of a woven fabric is a 45-degree angle between the lengthwise and crosswise grain lines.

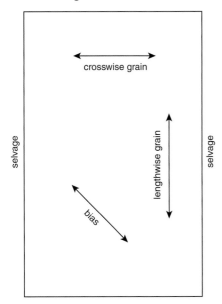

Straight & Bias Grain Lines

- **Mitered Corners:** Matching borders or turning bindings at a 45-degree angle at corners.
- **Patchwork:** A general term for the completed blocks or quilts that are made from smaller shapes sewn together.

- **Pattern:** This may refer to the design of a fabric or to the written instructions for a particular quilt design.
- **Piecing:** The act of sewing smaller pieces and/or units of a block or quilt together.

  Paper or foundation piecing is sewing fabric to a paper or cloth foundation in a certain order.

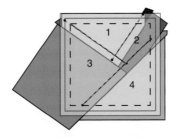

Foundation Piecing

String or chain piecing is sewing pieces together in a continuous string without clipping threads between sections.

String or Chain Piecing

- **Pressing:** Pressing is the process of placing the iron on the fabric, lifting it off the fabric and placing it down in another location to flatten seams or crease fabric without sliding the iron across the fabric.

  Quilters do not usually use steam when pressing, since it can easily distort fabric shapes.

  Generally, seam allowances are pressed toward the darker fabric in quilting so that they do not show through the lighter fabric.

  Seams are pressed in opposite directions where seams are being joined to allow seams to butt against each other and to distribute bulk.

Seams are pressed open when multiple seams come together in one place.

If you have a question about pressing direction, consult a comprehensive quilting guide for guidance.

- **Quilt (noun):** A sandwich of two layers of fabric with a third insulating material between them that is then stitched together with the edges covered or bound.
- **Quilt (verb):** Stitching several layers of fabric materials together with a decorative design. Stippling, cross-hatch, channel, in-the-ditch, free-motion, allover and meandering are all terms for quilting designs.

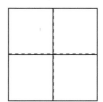

Meandering   **Stitch-in-the-ditch**

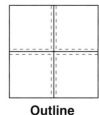

Channel   **Outline**

- **Quilt Sandwich:** A layer of insulating material between a quilt's top and back fabric.
- **Rotary Cutting:** Using a rotary cutting blade and straightedge to cut fabric.
- **Sashing:** Strips of fabric sewn between blocks to separate or set off the designs.
- **Subcut:** A second cutting of rotary-cut strips that makes the basic shapes used in block and quilt construction.
- **Template:** A pattern made from a sturdy material which is then used to cut shapes for patchwork and appliqué quilting. ●

Special Thanks

Please join us in thanking the talented designers
whose work is featured in this collection.

Lyn Brown
Village by the Sea, page 3

Holly Daniels
Color Perfect, page 12

Bev Getschel
Checks & Balances, page 25

Chris Malone
Scrap Basket Table Runner, page 16
The Whole Box of Crayons, page 8

Tricia Lynn Maloney
Cakes, page 21

Lolita Newman
Welcome to the Neighborhood, page 38

Nancy Scott
Nose-Diving Quilt, page 30
Simply Sophisticated Table Runner, page 34

Supplies

We would like to thank the following manufacturers who provided
materials to our designers to make sample projects for this book.

Village by the Sea, page 3: Batiks from Hoffman California-International Fabrics.

Color Perfect, page 12: Soft & Bright® batting from The Warm Company.

Cakes, page 21: Colorfully Creative and Confetti Cottons fabrics from Riley Blake Designs.

Checks & Balances, page 25: Batiks from Hoffman California-International Fabrics; Nature-Fil™ bamboo blend batting from Fairfield.

Annie's® *Stash-Busting Quilts* is published by Annie's, 306 East Parr Road, Berne, IN 46711. Printed in USA. Copyright © 2017 Annie's. All rights reserved. This publication may not be reproduced in part or in whole without written permission from the publisher.

RETAIL STORES: If you would like to carry this publication or any other Annie's publications, visit AnniesWSL.com.

Every effort has been made to ensure that the instructions in this publication are complete and accurate. We cannot, however, take responsibility for human error, typographical mistakes or variations in individual work. Please visit AnniesCustomerService.com to check for pattern updates.

ISBN: 978-1-59012-812-1

1 2 3 4 5 6 7 8 9

Here's your answer to the scrap dilemma.

If your scraps are out of control and you need help finding ways to use them, but you're not a scrappy quilter, here's the solution. *Stash-Busting Quilts* is a unique collection of patterns for the quilter with lots of stash and scraps but who doesn't like the scrappy look. Let our designers show you how to make the most of small amounts of fabric and put those gorgeous morsels of prime fabric to work. Here you'll find 9 scrap possibilities that will change how you feel about scraps.

EAN ISBN: 978-1-59012-812-1

9 781590 128121   51299

UPC U.S. $12.99 CANADA $15.99

7 32526 41518 0

PRINTED IN USA
AnniesCraftStore.com

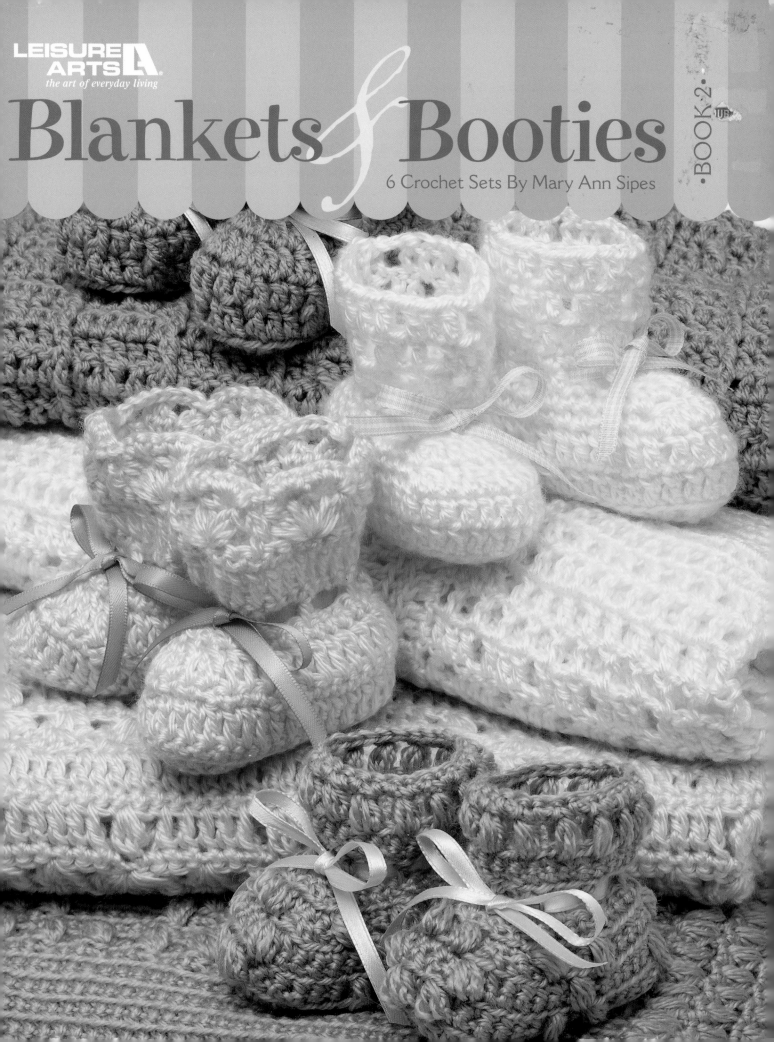

LEISURE ARTS
the art of everyday living

Blankets & Booties

· BOOK · 2 ·

6 Crochet Sets By Mary Ann Sipes